CONTEÚDO DIGITAL PARA ALUNOS

Cadastre-se e transforme seus estudos em uma experiência única de aprendizado:

1. Entre na página de cadastro:
https://sistemas.editoradobrasil.com.br/cadastro

2. Além dos seus dados pessoais e dos dados de sua escola, adicione ao cadastro o código do aluno, que garantirá a exclusividade do seu ingresso à plataforma.

2010359A1218921

3. Depois, acesse:
https://leb.editoradobrasil.com.br/
e navegue pelos conteúdos digitais de sua coleção :D

Lembre-se de que esse código, pessoal e intransferível, é valido por um ano. Guarde-o com cuidado, pois é a única maneira de você acessar os conteúdos da plataforma.

BRINCANDO
COM INGLÊS

**ENSINO FUNDAMENTAL
ANOS INICIAIS**

RENATO MENDES CURTO JÚNIOR
Licenciado em Letras
Certificado de proficiência em Língua Inglesa pela Universidade de Michigan e TOEFL
Autor de livros de educação a distância
Professor de Língua Inglesa e Portuguesa na rede particular de ensino desde 1986

ANNA CAROLINA GUIMARÃES
Licenciada em pedagogia
Especialista em Educação Infantil e anos iniciais
Especialista em neuropsicopedagogia
Coordenadora pedagógica de Educação básica

CIBELE MENDES
Mestre em Educação
Licenciada em Pedagogia
Certificado de proficiência em Língua Inglesa pela Fluency Academy
Coordenadora pedagógica de Educação Infantil aos Anos Finais do Ensino Fundamental

Editora do Brasil

Dados Internacionais de Catalogação na Publicação (CIP)
(Câmara Brasileira do Livro, SP, Brasil)

Curto Júnior, Renato Mendes
　　Brincando com inglês 5 : ensino fundamental : anos iniciais / Renato Mendes Curto Júnior, Anna Carolina Guimarães, Cibele Mendes. -- 5. ed. -- São Paulo : Editora do Brasil, 2024. -- (Brincando com)

　　ISBN 978-85-10-09494-8 (aluno)
　　ISBN 978-85-10-09495-5 (professor)

　　1. Língua inglesa (Ensino fundamental)
I. Guimarães, Anna Carolina. II. Mendes, Cibele.
III. Título. IV. Série.

24-197236　　　　　　　　　　　　CDD-372.652

Índices para catálogo sistemático:

1. Língua inglesa : Ensino fundamental 372.652
Cibele Maria Dias - Bibliotecária - CRB-8/9427

© Editora do Brasil S.A., 2024
Todos os direitos reservados

Direção-geral: Paulo Serino de Souza

Diretoria editorial: Felipe Ramos Poletti
Gerência editorial de conteúdo didático: Erika Caldin
Gerência editorial de produção e design: Ulisses Pires
Supervisão de design: Aurélio Gadini Camilo
Supervisão de arte: Abdonildo José de Lima Santos
Supervisão de revisão: Elaine Cristina da Silva
Supervisão de iconografia: Léo Burgos
Supervisão de digital: Priscila Hernandez
Supervisão de controle e planejamento editorial: Roseli Said
Supervisão de direitos autorais: Luciana Sposito
Supervisão editorial: Carla Felix Lopes e Diego Mata
Edição: Danuza D. Gonçalves, Graziele Arantes Mattiuzzi, Natália Feulo, Nayra Simões e Sheila Fabre
Assistência editorial: Igor Gonçalves, Julia do Nascimento, Natalia Soeda e Pedro Andrade Bezerra
Revisão: 2014 Soluções Editoriais, Alexander Siqueira, Andréia Andrade, Beatriz Dorini, Bianca Oliveira, Gabriel Ornelas, Giovana Sanches, Jonathan Busato, Júlia Castello, Maisa Akazawa, Mariana Paixão, Martin Gonçalves, Rita Costa, Rosani Andreani, Sandra Fernandes e Yasmin Fonseca
Pesquisa iconográfica: Maria Santos e Selma Nagano
Tratamento de imagens: Robson Mereu
Projeto gráfico: Caronte Design
Capa: Caronte Design
Imagem de capa: Thais Castro
Edição de arte: Camila de Camargo e Marcos Gubiotti
Ilustrações: André Aguiar, Desenhorama, Evandro Marenda, Lais Bicudo, Luiz Lentini, Marcelo Azalim, Marcos de Mello, Paulo Borges e Valter Paulo Ferrari
Editoração eletrônica: Abel Design
Licenciamentos de textos: Cinthya Utiyama, Ingrid Granzotto, Renata Garbellini e Solange Rodrigues
Controle e planejamento editorial: Ana Fernandes, Bianca Gomes, Juliana Gonçalves, Maria Trofino, Terezinha Oliveira e Valéria Alves

5ª edição / 1ª impressão, 2024
Impresso na Hawaii Gráfica e Editora

Avenida das Nações Unidas, 12901
Torre Oeste, 20º andar
São Paulo, SP – CEP: 04578-910
Fone: + 55 11 3226-0211

www.editoradobrasil.com.br

APRESENTAÇÃO

Querido aluno, querida aluna,

Este material foi elaborado para que você aprenda inglês de forma divertida, por meio de atividades estimulantes e desafiadoras, com o intuito de transformar a sala de aula em um espaço para praticar a língua inglesa brincando!

Nesta nova versão do **Brincando com Inglês**, cada aula será uma nova experiência, e você não vai querer parar de aprender. Vamos começar?

Os autores

CONHEÇA SEU LIVRO

Boas-vindas à nova edição do **Brincando com Inglês**!

LET'S START!
No início de cada volume, esta seção resgata conhecimentos prévios e apresenta atividades lúdicas que possibilitam a preparação para os novos conteúdos.

COMPREHENSION
As atividades desta seção visam à compreensão do texto visto na abertura da unidade.

VOCABULARY
Apresenta o vocabulário das palavras vistas na unidade, com a tradução em língua portuguesa.

LET'S PLAY
Seção relacionada aos conceitos propostos e à temática da unidade. Você encontrará atividades lúdicas, como diagramas de palavras, jogos de relacionar, jogos de erros, desafios etc.

GOOD DEED
Apresenta atividades temáticas de cunho social e ético relacionadas ao assunto de cada unidade. Aborda as competências gerais e socioemocionais da BNCC e as atividades feitas em grupos ou duplas.

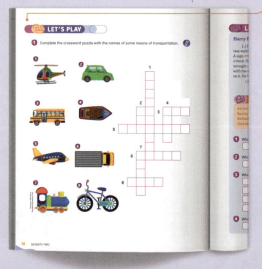

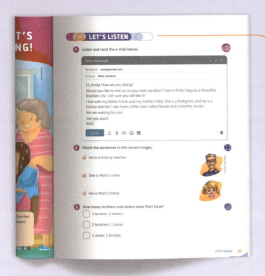

LET'S SING!
Músicas para você cantar e praticar o vocabulário visto na unidade de forma lúdica e divertida.

LET'S LISTEN
Seção com atividades que têm como objetivo a compreensão de áudios.

GRAMMAR POINT
Boxe com conteúdos gramaticais para que você compreenda a estrutura estudada e sistematize escrita e oralidade.

LITERARY TIME
Boxe com pequenos textos literários, de gêneros e suportes variados, para incentivar a leitura, aumentar o vocabulário e trabalhar a compreensão textual.

STICKERS
Adesivos para colar em algumas atividades.

CELEBRATIONS
Cartonados com atividades relacionadas a datas comemorativas.

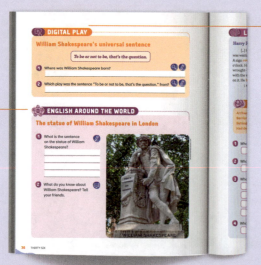

DIGITAL PLAY
Seção que trabalha atividades com o uso de tecnologia: filmagem, fotos, uso de apps e jogos *on-line*.

ENGLISH AROUND THE WORLD
Seção que contempla a Dimensão Intercultural da Língua Inglesa, trabalhando elementos da cultura em que se fala o idioma como língua oficial ou franca. Também são estudados os aspectos interculturais de outros países.

LET'S HAVE FUN
Seção que contém atividades variadas cuja proposta é desenvolver o estudo da língua inglesa com atividades práticas, ampliando o conhecimento e o vocabulário trabalhado.

AFTER THIS UNIT I CAN
Seção de autoavaliação e acompanhamento processual pelo aluno e professor.

ÍCONES

ADESIVO	COLAR	FALAR OU CONVERSAR
APONTAR	COLORIR	LIGAR/RELACIONAR
CANTAR	CONTAR	MARCAR
CARTONADO	DESENHAR	RECORTAR
CIRCULAR	ENCONTRAR/PESQUISAR	TRAÇAR/ESCREVER

CONTENTS

LET'S START! 8

UNIT 1
Fun, hobbies, and games! 19

UNIT 2
The seasons of the year 31

UNIT 3
Different cities 41

UNIT 4
Matt's family 51

UNIT 5
Means of transportation 63

UNIT 6
At the school cafeteria 75

UNIT 7
A message to a friend 87

UNIT 8
Traveling with friends 97

REVIEW 107

GLOSSARY 120

INDEX

   SONGS 127

   LISTENINGS 127

CELEBRATIONS 129

STICKERS 145

LET'S START!

1 Look at the picture and write a sentence about the importance of exercise for the health.

_____
_____

2 Find and circle the words in the wordsearch.

Art * History * Math * Portuguese
Geography * English * Science

```
S C I E N C E D I U S C D D P
G F U S F V S F H S F G S F O
A G H A G B A X I A G E A G R
L M A T H N L H S L H O L H T
E D E D K C A R T D D G S O U
C D I Y D C F D O D D R D D G
G I W I C S V E R U Z A T Y U
J G H A G B A G Y A G P H A E
L R N T W A H Q T L H H T L S
D D E N G L I S H D D Y H D E
E R H C W N W D L Z R H E S I
O R Q H G L W X Q M L H O Q D
```

3 Paste the stickers to complete the occupations album.

4 Write A or AN before the following words.

a)
_____ nurse

b)
_____ actor

c)
_____ doctor

d)
_____ architect

e)
_____ fireman

f)
_____ athlete

5 What school subjects are they? Unscramble the letters.

a) EOAYHPRGG

____

b) EIHSLGN

____

c) THMA

____

d) YOIHSTR

____

e) LPAHCYIS OIAUEDCTN

____

f) ESCCNIE

____

g) TRA

____

6 What musical instruments are these? Write them down.

a) 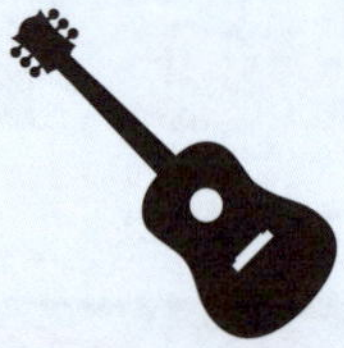

____

b) 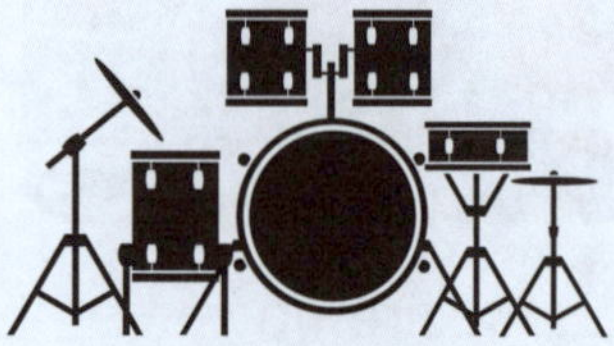

____

c) 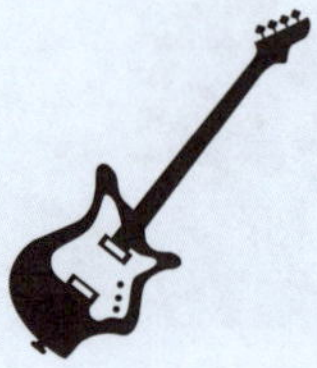

____

d) 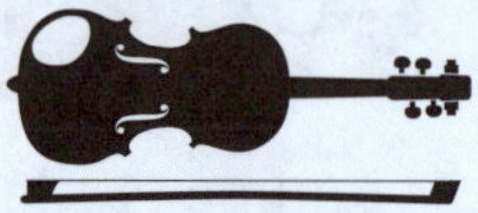

____

e) 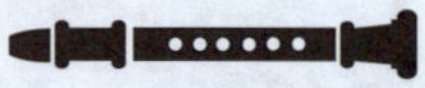

____

f) 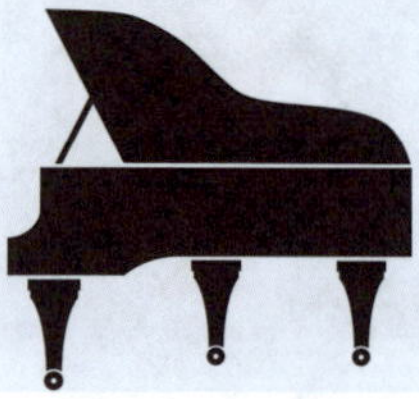

____

Ilustrações: Aliaksandr Radzko/Shutterstock.com

7 Complete the sequence of the ordinal numbers.

a) _____ – first
b) _____ – second
c) _____ – third
d) _____ – fourth
e) _____ – fifth

f) _____ – sixth
g) _____ – seventh
h) _____ – eighth
i) _____ – ninth
j) _____ – tenth

8 Make a list of your favorite music genres.

My favorite music genres are:

ELEVEN 11

9 Complete the crossword puzzle.

chicken * orange * fruits
pasta * cafeteria * vegetables

10 Complete the sentences with the correct question word.

What ✻ When ✻ Who ✻ Where

a)

_____ can you find trees, bushes, and flowers?

In a park.

b)

_____ are these people?

These people are my father, my mother, my sister, and my brother.

c)

_____ is there in your locker?

There is a backpack, a doll, a bicycle, a top, a coat, and a pair of sneakers.

d)

_____ was the clock invented?

The clock was invented a long time ago.

11 Write the numbers in full or numeric form.

a) 84: _____
b) sixty: _____
c) 25: _____
d) ninety: _____
e) 100: _____
f) fourteen: _____

g) 38: _____
h) seventy-one: _____
i) 42: _____
j) sixty-three: _____
k) 55: _____
l) ninety-nine: _____

12 Complete with the verb **to be**: AM, IS, or ARE.

a)

I _____ happy.

d)

My husband and my son _____ tall.

b)

He _____ my father.

e)

She _____ a musician.

c)

My friends _____ American.

f)

It _____ my bike.

14 FOURTEEN

13 Connect the dots, color the objects, and write the name of the sports.

C_____

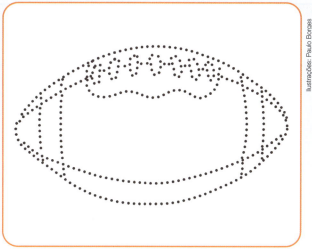

F_____

14 Complete the sentences according to the pictures. Use THIS or THAT.

a)

_____ is my house.

c)

I want _____ T-shirt.

b)

_____ flower is beautiful.

d)

_____ food is delicious.

FIFTEEN 15

15 Create a list of the clothes and shoes you wear to go to school. Draw and write the correct word.

a)

_____

b)

_____

c)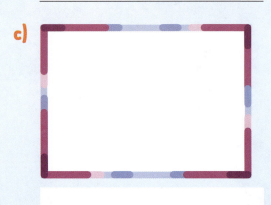

_____

d)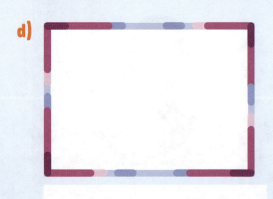

_____

e)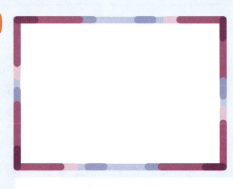

_____

f)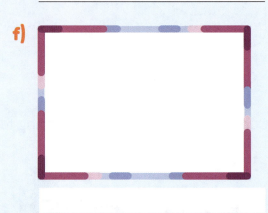

_____

g)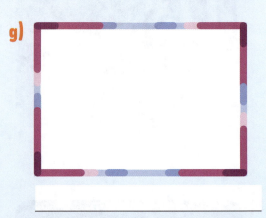

_____

h)

_____

16 Write sentences according to the pictures. Describe the food and the scene.

a)

_____
_____

b)

_____
_____

c)

_____
_____

d)

_____
_____

17 Choose one photo from activity 16 and write a warning sentence about the importance of healthy eating habits.

_____
_____

18 Choose the best option according to the picture.

a) The tree is _____ the rocks.
- [ ] between
- [ ] near
- [ ] in front of

b) The owl is _____ the tree branch.
- [ ] near
- [ ] on
- [ ] between

c) The car is _____ the house.
- [ ] at
- [ ] in
- [ ] in front of

d) They are _____ the bus stop.
- [ ] between
- [ ] at
- [ ] in front of

UNIT 1
FUN, HOBBIES, AND GAMES!

Hello, Abbie! What's up? What's this in your hand?

I'm fine! Oh, it is my flute! I love to play it in my **free time**. And you? What do you like to do **for fun**?

I **enjoy movies**, **roller skating**, and **reading books**.

Hello, girls! I've just played my favorite sport: soccer. At night, I will dance with my family!

Nice! I would like to have more time to do all the things I love! Picnics, drawing ...

Ride a bike, play with my cat, **travel**...

VOCABULARY

Enjoy (to enjoy): gostar, curtir.
For fun: para se divertir.
Free time: tempo livre.
Movies: filmes/cinema.

Nice: ótimo, legal.
Reading books: ler livros.
Roller skating (to roller skate): andar de patins.
Travel (to travel): viajar.

NINETEEN 19

COMPREHENSION

1 Mark the characters' favorite things to do according to the dialogue: (H) for Harry, (A) for Abbie, or (E) for Eloise.

- to play the flute ☐
- to watch a movie ☐
- to play soccer ☐
- to have a picnic ☐
- to roller skate ☐
- to read books ☐
- to travel ☐
- to dance ☐
- to draw ☐
- to ride a bike ☐
- to play with the cat ☐

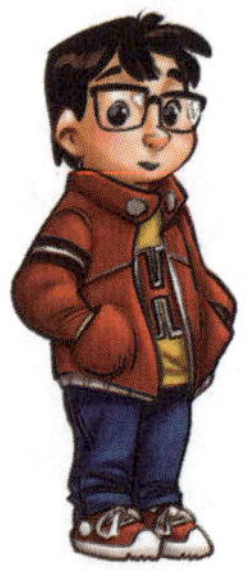

Harry

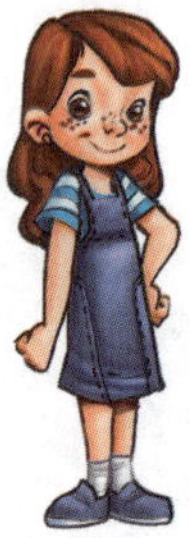

Abbie

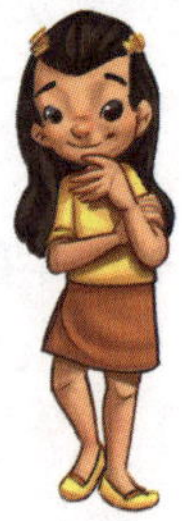

Eloise

Ilustrações: Paulo Borges

2 What does Eloise like to do for fun?

____

____

____

3 What is Harry's favorite sport?

____

LET'S PLAY

1 Read the sentences and mark the corresponding picture with **X**.

a) Sarah is roller skating in the park.

b) Oliver is playing video game with his friend.

c) Roberta likes to read books.

d) Evie likes to go fishing with her father.

e) Matt plays soccer every day.

f) George is skating in the park with his brother.

ABC GRAMMAR POINT

Verb TO BE – question form

Am I hungry?

Are you my friend?

Is he Matt?

Is she Eloise?

Is it a car?

Are we sisters?

Are you happy?

Are they friends?

LET'S PLAY

1 Complete the sentences with the correct form of the verb **to be** (**am**, **is**, or **are**).

a) _____ Jane a nurse?

b) _____ Suzy and Mary sisters?

c) _____ you from Italy?

d) _____ Peter a teacher?

2 Read the sentences and paste the correct sticker.

a) Are they cats? No, they are dogs.

c) Is she a teacher? No, she is a doctor.

b) Is it a notebook? No, it is a laptop.

d) Is he a kid? No, he is an adult.

3 Put the words in order and form questions. Follow the example.

> Olivia Rodrigo / singer / your / favorite / is / ?
> *Is Olivia Rodrigo your favorite singer?*

a) good / is / Neymar / player / a / soccer / ?
_____

b) are / student / good / a / you / ?
_____

c) good / a / actor / is / Noah Schnapp / ?
_____

4 Write sentences using the verb **to be** in the question form. Follow the example.

> I + beautiful ⟶ Am I beautiful?

a) He + hungry
_____

b) You + happy
_____

TWENTY-THREE 23

5 Find the words in the wordsearch and write them in the blanks. Then choose one word and write a sentence with it.

a)

_____

d)

_____

b)

_____

e)

_____

c)

_____

D	E	I	D	L	F	D	U	I	D	Q	C
S	W	I	M	M	I	N	G	G	A	F	V
A	Q	H	A	G	S	A	G	H	N	G	B
L	H	T	L	J	H	L	H	T	C	N	H
D	D	E	D	D	I	D	D	E	I	J	C
R	E	A	D	I	N	G	D	I	N	D	Q
S	F	G	S	F	G	H	F	B	G	F	V
A	Y	H	A	G	B	A	G	H	A	G	B
L	H	S	K	A	T	I	N	G	L	H	N
F	D	E	G	D	B	D	U	X	D	A	C

_____

 **GOOD DEED**

Leisure activities improve our quality of life!

Check out a few reasons why it is important to do leisure activities:

* They reduce stress;
* They improve quality of life;
* They build relationships and friendships;
* They are fun!

What leisure activities do you like? Write them down and draw them here.

LET'S SING!

Girls and boys come out to play

Girls and boys **come out** to play,
the **moon** does **shine** as **bright** as day.
Leave your **supper** and leave your **sleep**,
and come with your **playfellows** into the **street**.
Come with a **whoop**, come with a call,
come with a good will or not at all.
Up the **ladder** and down the **wall**,
a **halfpenny** roll will serve us all.

Nursery rhyme

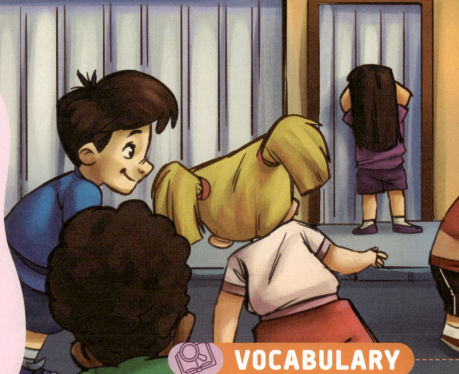

VOCABULARY

Bright: claro(a).
Come out (to come out): saiam (sair).
Halfpenny: centavo.
Ladder: escada.
Leave (to leave): deixem (deixar).
Moon: Lua.
Playfellow(s): amigo(s), companheiro(s) de brincadeiras.
Shine (to shine): brilha (brilhar).
Sleep: sono.
Street: rua.
Supper: ceia, jantar.
Wall: parede.
Whoop: uhul (grito de comemoração).

 **DIGITAL PLAY**

Let's play charades!

Guess the games, hobbies, or activities through mime.

Search and choose a fun hobby or sport, and write the word in English.

LET'S LISTEN

1 Listen to the sentences and complete them with the correct activities from the box.

> painting * fishing * take pictures * play video games

a) Abbie likes to _____ on weekends.

b) Sophie loves to _____ with a special camera.

c) Oliver goes _____ with his father every Sunday at the river.

d) Evie loves _____ canvas with flowers and pets.

2 Listen to the dialogue and answer the questions.

a) Who is good at playing video games?
☐ Matt.   ☐ Abbie.   ☐ George.   ☐ Evie.

b) Who prefers to roller skate in the park?
☐ George.   ☐ Matt.   ☐ Evie.   ☐ Oliver.

3 Circle Oliver's favorite leisure activities and mark **X** at Evie's favorite one.

LITERARY TIME

Let's read a Calvin and Hobbes comic strip!

VOCABULARY

Another: outro.
Can: posso/consigo (poder/conseguir).
Contemplative: contemplativo.
Go (to go): ir.

Really: realmente.
Sport: esporte.
Sure: claro/com certeza.
Want (to want): quer (querer).

1 Does Calvin like fishing?
- ☐ No, he doesn't like it.
- ☐ Yes, he likes it.

2 What is the humor in the comic strip?
- ☐ Calvin fishes in a different way.
- ☐ Calvin fishes like everybody else.

3 The way that Calvin is fishing is...
- ☐ calm.
- ☐ agressive.

ENGLISH AROUND THE WORLD

How children have fun in the USA, England, and New Zealand?

Look at the pictures and research the question. Then, write what activities, fun, and games you found in your search.

_____
_____
_____
_____
_____
_____
_____

AFTER THIS UNIT I CAN

	😊	😐	☹
Identify and use nouns.			
Identify and use adjectives.			
Understand the vocabulary of hobbies, games, and fun.			
Use the verb **to be**.			
Understand cultural differences among countries.			
Make the use of multiple languages.			

UNIT 2
THE SEASONS OF THE YEAR

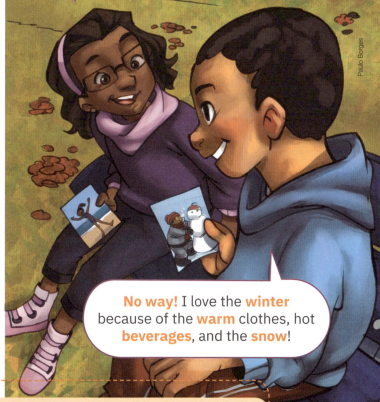

VOCABULARY

Beach: praia.
Beverage(s): bebida(s).
Fall: outono.
I can't wait: Mal posso esperar.
Leaves: folhas.
No way!: Nem pensar!
Snow: neve.
Spring: primavera.
Summer: verão.
Warm: quente.
Weather: clima.
Winter: inverno.

COMPREHENSION

1 What are the kids talking about?

_____

_____

2 Look at the pictures and answer.

a) What is Sophie's favorite season? Circle.

b) What is George's favorite season? Make a triangle around the corresponding picture.

Winter

Fall

Summer

Spring

LET'S PLAY

1 Read the descriptions and write the correct season.

a) There are lots of leaves on the ground.
_____

b) There are green trees and many flowers.
_____

c) There are cold temperatures and snow.
_____

d) There are hot temperatures and sunny days.
_____

2 Paste the stickers with the corresponding sentence from activity 1.

a)

b)

c)

d)

THIRTY-THREE 33

ABC GRAMMAR POINT

Verb TO BE – Negative form

I **am not** Sophie. I am Lilly.

You **are not** an adult. You are a kid.

He **is not** George. He is Nico.

She **is not** Abbie. She is Amie.

It **is not** a tablet. It is a cell phone.

We **are not** sisters. We are friends.

You **are not** sad. You are happy.

They **are not** cats. They are dogs.

I	am not
You	are not
He	is not
She	is not
It	is not
We	are not
You	are not
They	are not

LET'S PLAY

1 Unscramble the words. Pay attention to the negative form of the verb **to be**.

a) tall | a | I | boy | not | am

_____

b) girl | a | You | curious | not | are

_____

c) not | We | bad | are | students

_____

d) sister | quiet | a | not | is | She

_____

2 Choose words from the box and write 3 sentences using the negative form of the verb **to be**.

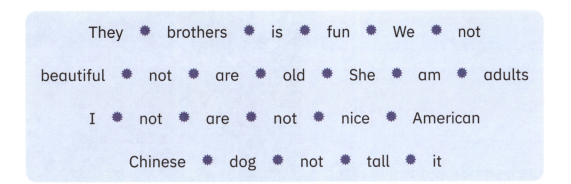

Sentence 1

_____

Sentence 2

_____

Sentence 3

_____

DIGITAL PLAY

William Shakespeare's universal sentence

To be or not to be, that's the question.

1. Where was William Shakespeare born?
   _____

2. Which play was the sentence "To be or not to be, that's the question." from?
   _____

ENGLISH AROUND THE WORLD

The statue of William Shakespeare in London

1. What is the sentence on the statue of William Shakespeare?
   _____
   _____
   _____
   _____

2. What do you know about William Shakespeare? Tell your friends.

Five little snowmen

Five little **snowmen standing in a line**,
one, two, three, four, five. So fine.
Melt in the sunshine with a **sigh**.
We'll see you next year, bye-bye!

Four little snowmen standing in a line,
one, two, three, four. So fine.
Melt in the sunshine with a sigh.
We'll see you next year, bye-bye!

Three little snowmen standing in a line,
one, two, three. So fine.
Melt in the sunshine with a sigh.
We'll see you next year, bye-bye!

Two little snowmen standing in a line,
one, two. So fine.
Melt in the sunshine with a sigh.
We'll see you next year, bye-bye!

One little **snowman** standing in a line,
one. So fine.
Melt in the sunshine with a sigh.
We'll see you next year, bye-bye!

Nursery rhyme.

LET'S SING!

VOCABULARY

In a line: em fila.
Melt (to melt): derretem (derreter).
Sigh: suspiro.
Snowman (snowmen): boneco de neve (bonecos de neve).
Standing (to stand): de pé.

LET'S LISTEN

1 Listen and circle the correct word.

a) Today is a **spring**/**winter** day.

b) William does not have **a coat**/**gloves**.

c) Evie saw the **newspaper**/**weather forecast**.

d) Oliver says to be **outside**/**inside**.

e) Chloe is a very **nice**/**kind** girl.

2 Listen again and write **T** (true) or **F** (false).

a) ☐ Everybody is worried about the winter.

b) ☐ One kid thinks that it will snow.

c) ☐ Kids don't enter the school.

d) ☐ Kids are friends because they take care of each other.

3 What do they like to do? Listen carefully and match the parts of the sentences

a) It's summer. Abbie likes — drinking hot chocolate and playing games.

b) It's winter. George enjoys — to go to the beach with her family.

c) It's fall. Oliver loves it — to collect flowers everywhere.

d) It's spring. Evie loves — because there is a lot of fruit.

LITERARY TIME

The ant and the grasshopper

In a **field** one summer day, a grasshopper was **hopping about**, singing. An ant **passed by**, **bearing** along an **ear of corn**.

"Come and **chat** with me instead of **working hard**!"

"I am helping to **lay up** food for the winter, and I recommend you do the same."

"Why **bother** with winter? We have **plenty of** food at present."

When the winter came, the grasshopper had no food and found itself **dying** of **hunger**, while the ants had the food they'd collected during the summer.

Then the grasshopper learned: It is best to prepare for the days of **necessity**.

Aesop fable. Adapted.

VOCABULARY

Bearing (to bear): carregando (carregar).
Bother (to bother): incomodar(-se).
Chat (to chat): converse (conversar).
Dying (to die): morrendo (morrer).
Ear of corn: espiga de milho.
Field: campo.
Hopping about (to hop about): saltitando (saltitar).
Hunger: fome.
Lay up (to lay up): juntar.
Necessity: necessidade.
Passed by (to pass by): passou por (passar por).
Plenty of: de sobra.
Working hard (to work hard): trabalhar duro (trabalhar duro).

Who is the ant? Who is the grasshopper? Look and match.

a)

b)

Grasshopper

Ant

LET'S HAVE FUN

1 What's your favorite season? What do you like to do in it? Write and draw.

My favorite season is _____

I love it because _____

I like to _____

AFTER THIS UNIT I CAN

	☺	😐	☹
Identify the seasons of the year.			
Identify adjectives to describe the weather.			
Identify and use the verb **to be** in the negative form.			
Recognize the importance of William Shakespeare to the world.			
Reflect on the importance of having fair attitudes.			

UNIT 3
DIFFERENT CITIES

Hey, William! What's up? Welcome to Toronto!

*Hi, Matt, thanks. I'm **excited** to **get to know** the **city**! What are our **plans**?*

*I'll **show** you the **museum**, the **library**, the **park**, the **stadium**, the **tower**, and the **lake**!*

***Awesome**! We'll have **a few days** to **enjoy** the city!*

VOCABULARY

A few days: uns dias/alguns dias.
Awesome: incrível.
City: cidade.
Enjoy (to enjoy): aproveitar (aproveitar).
Excited: animado(a).
Get to know (to get to know): conhecer.
Lake: lago.

Library: biblioteca.
Museum: museu.
Park: parque.
Plan(s): plano(s).
Show (to show): mostrar.
Stadium: estádio.
Tower: torre.

COMPREHENSION

1 Where do Matt and William meet?

☐ In the countryside.   ☐ In the city.

2 How is William feeling about the visit to Toronto?

_____

3 Look at Matt's map and mark **X** at the mall, the museum, the library, the school, and the park.

LET'S LISTEN

1 Listen and complete the dialogue using the words from the box.

map * bakery * library * museum * store * drugstore * movie theater

Matt: Hey, William, look! This is our neighborhood _____.

William: Nice! Where's the _____?

Matt: The bakery is on Saint Sebastian Street. It's in front of the shoe _____.

William: Cool! And where's the _____?

Matt: The library is on Bela Vista Street. It's next to the _____.

William: Great! Where is the _____?

Matt: The museum is on Main Street. It's between the _____ and the mall.

2 Mark an **X** at the locations on the list.

* The lake
* The park
* The tower
* The building

3 Look at the neighborhood map Matt shows William. Listen to the dialogue again and trace the path.

GRAMMAR POINT

Prepositions of place and directions

1. The house is **on** the tree.

2. The flower is **between** the tree and the ladder.

3. The squirrel is **in front of** the tree house.

4. The window is **next to** the door.

5. Turn right!

6. Go straight!

7. Turn left!

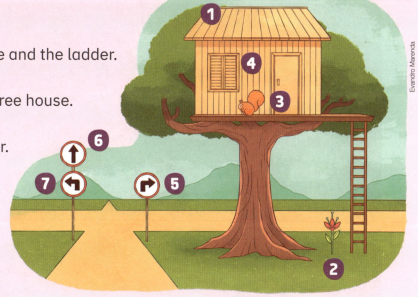

LET'S PLAY

1. Write what direction each traffic sign indicates.

a)

_____

b)

_____

c)

_____

2 Look at the map. Complete the sentences using the prepositions of place from the box.

On * Between * In front of * Next to

a) The supermarket is _____ the drugstore.

b) The cinema is not _____ the museum.

c) The stores are _____ the park and the school.

d) The bakery is _____ the Mary Ann street.

3 Draw a street in a separate sheet of paper. Read the descriptions and place the stickers in the correct place.

* The hospital is between the movie theater and the school.

* The supermarket is next to the school.

* The library is on the left of the movie theater.

LET'S SING!

Rig a jig jig

As I was **walking down** the street
down the street
down the street.
A very good friend
I happened to **meet**.
hi ho, hi ho, hi ho.

Rig a jig jig and **away** we go
away we go, away we go!
Rig a jig jig and away we go
hi ho, hi ho, hi ho!

Nursery rhyme.

VOCABULARY

Away: longe.
Meet (to meet): encontrar.
Walking down (to walk down): caminhando pela(o) (caminhar por).

DIGITAL PLAY

The reading and the imagination

Check how you prefer to do your readings. Write the names of the objects.

ENGLISH AROUND THE WORLD

The technology and social networks in the world

Most used social networks in the world in 2023

- Facebook – 2.9 billion (accounts)
- YouTube – 2.5 billion
- Instagram – 2 billion
- WhatsApp – 2 billion
- TikTok – 1 billion
- Snapchat – 635 million
- Twitter – 556 million

Fernanda Beling. As 10 [...]. *Oficina da Net*, [s. l.], 2023.

Write the names of the social networks that you use the most.

LITERARY TIME

Let's read a Garfield comic strip!

1 What did Garfield's owner say to him?

- [ ] They're going to another city.
- [ ] They're going to the farm.
- [ ] They're going to the beach.

2 What reaction was Garfield?

_____
_____

3 What is the element of humor present at the end of the strip?

- [ ] Garfield said he will be happy and excited on the farm.
- [ ] Garfield said he will still be bored, but now on the farm.

4 What do you like to do in the city? And on the farm? Write your answers.

a) In the city: _____

b) On the farm: _____

LET'S PLAY

1 Look at the flyer and complete the sentences correctly.

a) People are taking a tour _____ the tour bus. (in/on)

b) There is one bus _____ the flyer. (in/on)

c) _____ many people on the tour bus. (There is/There are)

d) They get _____ the tour bus at the bus stop. (at/on)

2 Look at the flyer and find the people. Then complete the sentences.

a) The girl in the purple and pink T-shirt is _____ a boy in blue and a kid in yellow.

b) The man in a green T-shirt is _____ the woman in the pink hat.

AFTER THIS UNIT I CAN

Talk about the importance of different cities.

Identify places and parts of cities.

Understand prepositions of place and direction.

Understand the importance of reading.

Understand information about digital culture and social networks.

COMPREHENSION

1. Read the sentences and fill in the blanks.
   a) Andy is Matt's _____.
   b) Patty is Matt's _____.
   c) Roy is Nanda's _____.
   d) James is Matt's _____.
   e) Austin is Roy's _____.
   f) Frank is Matt's _____.

2. Who is Nanda?
   ☐ Matt's sister.   ☐ Matt's cousin.

3. Who is Roy?
   He is Matt's _____.

4. Unscramble the letters and write the family members.
   a) faehtr
   _____
   b) gfrtahnedra
   _____
   c) srtise
   _____
   d) csiuon
   _____
   e) lncue
   _____
   f) ghtmdraoren
   _____
   g) utna
   _____
   h) rrotehb
   _____

ABC GRAMMAR POINT

Verb TO BE – affirmative form

I **am** Julia.

You **are** a student.

He **is** a father.

She **is** a mother.

It **is** a ball.

We **are** brothers.

You **are** happy.

They **are** cousins.

LET'S PLAY

1 Complete the sentences with the correct form of the verb **to be** (**am**, **is**, or **are**).

a) Peter _____ a doctor.

b) Suzy and Mary _____ students.

c) We _____ tall.

d) John _____ a teacher.

2 Draw your family tree and show it to your classmates. Use the words in the box.

> Grandmother ✲ Mother ✲ Brother ✲ Grandfather ✲ Father ✲ Sister ✲ Uncle ✲ Aunt ✲ Cousin

GOOD DEED

We should respect our family and the elders

Why should we respect the elders?

* Because we should treat others the way we would like to be treated.
* Because they love us.
* Because they are part of our family history.
* Because they teach us lots of things.
* Because they (and everyone) deserve it!

1 What does "respect the elders" mean to you? Choose the best options.

- [ ] love
- [ ] dislike
- [ ] selfishness
- [ ] kindness
- [ ] politeness
- [ ] rudeness

2 Make a collage about it on an extra sheet of paper.

Grandma's house

LET'S SING!

We are **walking**, walking, walking,
and we're talking, talking, talking,
in the rain, rain, rain,
on the way to Grandma's house.

Thunder's **crashing**, crashing, crashing,
we go **splashing**, splashing, splashing,
in the rain, rain, rain,
on the way to Grandma's house.

Now we're **dripping**, dripping, dripping,
and we're **tripping**, tripping, tripping,
in the rain,
rain, rain,
on the way to
Grandma's house.

And now **looking**, looking, looking,
at the **cookie**, cookie, cookie,
on the table, table, table,
here at Grandma's house.

Now it's yummy, yummy, yummy,
in my **tummy**, tummy, tummy,
and it's **warm**, warm, warm,
here at Grandma's house.

Original source: unknown.

VOCABULARY

Cookie: biscoito.
Crashing (to crash): estrondeando (estrondear).
Dripping (to drip): gotejando (gotejar).
Looking (to look): olhando (olhar).
On the way: a caminho.

Splashing (to splash): borrifando (borrifar).
Tripping (to trip): tropeçando (tropeçar).
Tummy: barriguinha.
Walking (to walk): caminhando (caminhar).
Warm: quente.

56   FIFTY-SIX

LET'S LISTEN

1 Listen and read the e-mail below.

New message

Recipient andy@email.com

Subject Next vacation

Hi, Andy! How are you doing?

Would you like to visit us on your next vacation? I live in Porto Seguro, a beautiful Brazilian city. I am sure you will like it!

I live with my father, Frank, and my mother, Patty. She is a firefighter, and he is a history teacher. I also have a little sister called Nanda and a brother, Austin.

We are waiting for you!

See you soon!
Matt.

Send

2 Match the sentences to the correct images.

a) He is a history teacher.

b) She is Matt's sister.

c) He is Matt's father.

3 How many brothers and sisters does Matt have?

☐ 1 brother, 2 sisters.

☐ 2 brothers, 1 sister.

☐ 1 sister, 1 brother.

FIFTY-SEVEN 57

4. Use the stickers to complete Matt's family tree.

LET'S LISTEN

1 Listen and complete with the verb **to be**.

New message

Hi, Andy! How are you?

I want to tell you a little bit more about me and my family. We live in Porto Seguro and both my mother Patty and my aunt Vilma _____ firefighters.

My aunt Christina is a wonderful cook.

My father _____ a history teacher and my uncle Oswald _____ a journalist. My uncle James _____ an athlete.

I have two cousins, Roy, who _____ five years old, and Celina, who _____ fourteen years old.

My grandpas, Louis and Kevin, are the same age. They are sixty-two years old, but my grandmas _____ younger. Grandma Molly is sixty years old and grandma Selma _____ fifty-nine years old.

All of them _____ very happy with your visit, Andy!

See you soon!

Matt.

---

2 Listen to the message again and choose the correct option.

a) Who is a wonderful cook?
- ☐ Christina is a wonderful cook.
- ☐ Vilma is a wonderful cook.

b) Which grandma is fifty-nine years old?
- ☐ Grandma Selma.
- ☐ Grandma Molly.

LITERARY TIME

The Berenstain Bears' family reunion

[...] Yes! We'll see Grizzly Gramps and Gran, of course, **Great--aunt** Min and Cousin Morse. Aunts and **uncles**, **nephews**, **nieces** will come **together** like **puzzle pieces**.

[...]

Stan Berenstain, Jan Berenstain and Mike Berenstain. *The Berenstain Bears' family reunion*. New York: HarperCollins, 2009.

VOCABULARY

Great-aunt: tia-avó.
Nephew(s): sobrinho(s).
Niece(s): sobrinha(s).
Piece(s): peça(s).
Puzzle: quebra-cabeça.
Together: juntos.
Uncle(s): tio(s).

1 List all the relatives mentioned in the text.
_____
_____

2 Who is Min? Choose correctly.
☐ The great-aunt.
☐ The niece.
☐ The grandmother.
☐ The cousin.

ENGLISH AROUND THE WORLD

The famous cartoon families

1 Write the name of the families described in the sentences.

a) They live in the Stone Age:

b) They are superheroes:

c) They are scary and different:

2 Search and write the names of 2 famous cartoon families around the world. Discover their names in English.

3 Now, write the names of all members of the 2 families mentioned and identify their relationship.

DIGITAL PLAY

Secret agent: let's create and decipher codes

Decipher the words hidden in the codes that indicate kinship.

a)
MOTHER

b)
UNCLE

c)
PARENTS

d)
SISTER

e)
FATHER

f)
SON

g)
BROTHER

h)
GRANDFATHER

AFTER THIS UNIT I CAN

- Identify family members, and talk about them.
- Understand and identify the degree of kinship.
- Talk about professions.
- Value the popular culture of films and cartoons from other countries and our country.
- Interpret and contextualize texts.
- Reflect on good respectful attitudes towards elderly people and family.

UNIT 5
MEANS OF TRANSPORTATION

At the museum of means of transportation…

"I had no idea there are so many different means of transportation! I liked to see so many **trains**, **subways**, **cars**, **buses**, **trucks**, and **motorbikes**!"

"Oh, really? I prefer the aquatic means of transportation: there are many kinds of **boats**. I would like to **sail someday**!"

"Sorry, but **flying** through the **sky** must be more **exciting**! I **would like** to fly in a **balloon** one day!"

"We can move by **land**, air, or **water**."

VOCABULARY

Balloon: balão.
Boat(s): barco(s).
Bus(es): ônibus.
Car(s): carro(s).
Exciting: emocionante.
Flying (to fly): voar.

Land: terra.
Motorbike(s): motocicleta(s).
Sail (to sail): velejar.
Sky: céu.
Someday: algum dia.

Subway(s): metrô(s).
Train(s): trem (trens).
Truck(s): caminhão (caminhões).
Water: água.
Would like: gostaria.

COMPREHENSION

1 Who prefers to move...

  a) by water? _____

  b) by air? _____

2 Where are the kids? _____

3 Look at the pictures, read, and say the means of transportation.

By land:

car   truck   bus   train

motorcycle   subway   bicycle

By air:

helicopter   plane   hot-air balloon

By water:

ship   boat   canoe

speedboat   ferry

DIGITAL PLAY

The fascinating New York subway

Research and mark the correct alternatives according to the New York subway.

☐ Works 24 hours.   ☐ 36 lines.   ☐ 500 lines.

ENGLISH AROUND THE WORLD

How the MetroCard Ticket works in New York

1 How much does a single MetroCard cost?
_____

2 What are the two options of MetroCard ticket?
_____

ABC GRAMMAR POINT

Modal – would like

It is used to make **polite requests**.

It is used as a synonym for **want**.

Observe:

I **would like** to sail someday.

I **would like** to fly through the sky.

I **would like** to take the subway.

LET'S PLAY

1 What means of transportation would they like to use? Observe the images and answer.

a)

Sophie would like to go by _____.

b)

Matt would like to go by _____.

2 What means of transportation would you like to use?

_____
_____
_____

GOOD DEED

Ecological Means of Transportation

We must warn people about the importance of ecological means of transportation.

Being eco-friendly will make you feel good! It pollutes less, improves your health, and is more sustainable.

Share this idea with your friends and family!

Which are the ecological means of transportation? Mark.

LET'S LISTEN

1 Listen and write the means of transportation into the appropriate column.

By land	By air	By water

LET'S SING!

The wheels on the bus

The **wheels** on the bus **go round** and round,
round and round, round and round.
The wheels on the bus go round and round,
all day long!

The **bell** on the bus goes "Ding, ding, ding!
Ding, ding, ding... ding, ding, ding!"
The bell on the bus goes "Ding, ding, ding!"
All day long!

The **wipers** on the bus go "**Swish**, swish, swish,
swish, swish, swish... swish, swish, swish!"
The wipers on the bus go "Swish, swish, swish!"
All day long!

The **driver** on the bus says, "**Any** more **fares**?
Any more fares? Any more fares?"
The driver on the bus says, "Any more fares?"
All day long! All day long!

Traditional nursery rhyme.

VOCABULARY

Any: algum(a).
Bell: sino.
Driver: motorista.
Fare(s): passagem (passagens).
Go round (to go round): giram (girar).
Swish (to swish): balançam (balançar, mover-se com um som suave).
Wheel(s): roda(s).
Wiper(s): limpador(es) de para-brisa.

LET'S LISTEN

1 Listen and complete the dialogue.

Matt: This park is really beautiful, guys. It is perfect to come by _____.

Evie: Yes, it is! I love to ride my bicycle. What about you, Eloise? What is your favorite means of transportation?

Eloise: I like to use the subway. It is fast and organized. Oliver and I always use the subway or the _____.

Oliver: Yes, it is really practical! But today we used the _____. It was easier.

Matt: Nice! There are so many types of transportation we can use… It is incredible we can move through _____, _____, and _____!

Evie: I would love to fly through the _____! It would be wonderful to fly in a _____. It looks so peaceful!

Eloise: I would love to cross the ocean in a _____. Like Titanic… It looks so romantic!

Oliver: I like to race! Driving a _____ or a _____ seems so exciting!

COMPREHENSION

1 Now, listen to the audio again and answer some questions.

a) What means of transportation does Oliver use to get to the park?
- ☐ Subway.
- ☐ Bus.
- ☐ Bicycle.

b) What means of transportation do Eloise and Oliver usually use? Circle it.

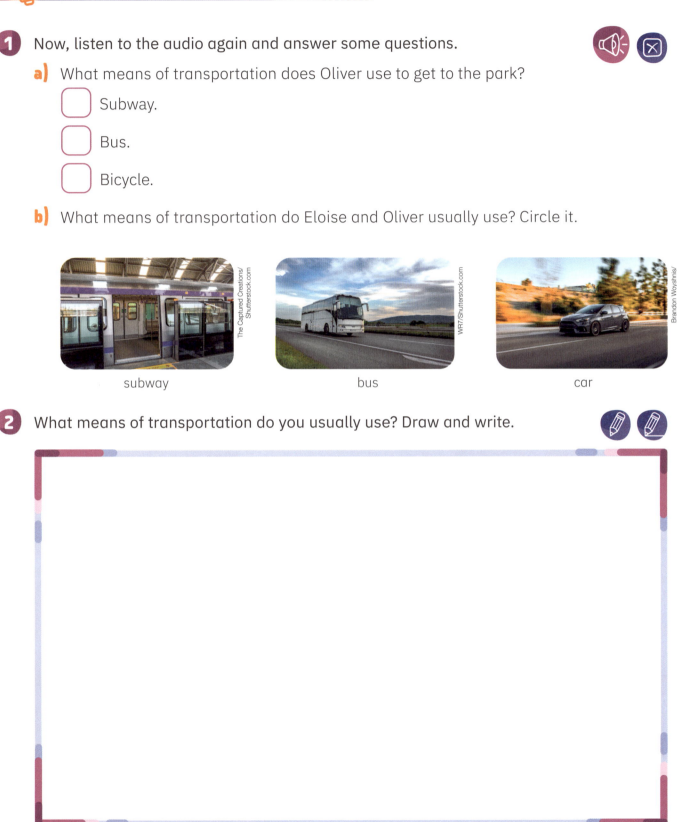

subway   bus   car

2 What means of transportation do you usually use? Draw and write.

LET'S PLAY

1 Complete the crossword puzzle with the names of some means of transportation.

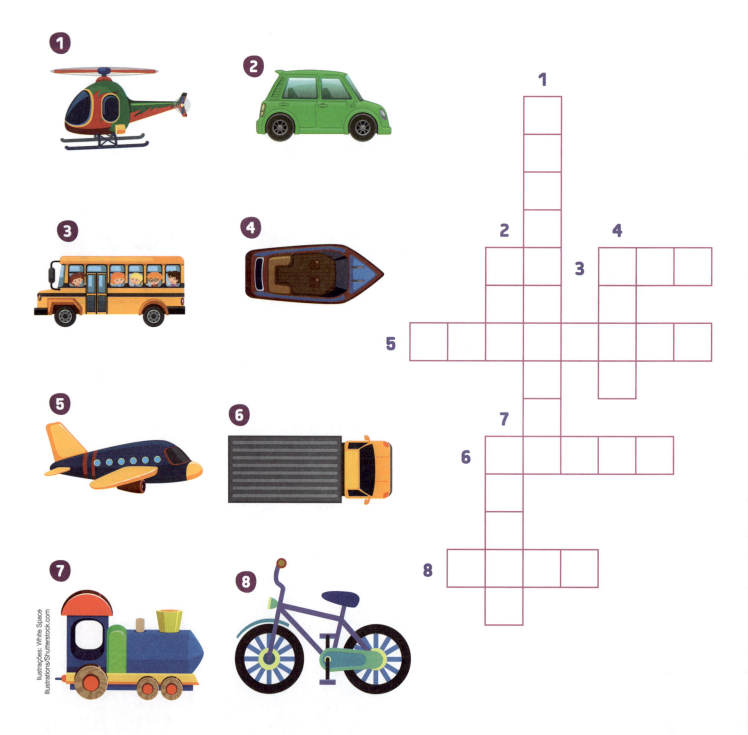

LITERARY TIME

Harry Potter and The Sorcerer's Stone

[...] He **opened** his eyes. A scarlet steam engine was waiting next to a platform packed with people. A sign **overhead** said Hogwarts Express, eleven o'clock. Harry **looked behind** him and saw a wrought-iron **archway** where the **barrier** had been, with the words Platform Nine and Three-Quarters on it. He **had done it**. [...]

J. K. Rowling. *Harry Potter and the Sorcerer's Stone*. Scotland: Scholastic, 1997. p. 88.

VOCABULARY

Archway: arco.
Barrier: barreira.
Behind: atrás.
Had done it: conseguiu (conseguir).
Looked (to look): olhou (olhar).
Opened (to open): abriu (abrir).
Overhead: aéreo, acima da cabeça.

1. What means of transportation is mentioned in the text?
   ☐ Car. ☐ Boat. ☐ Train. ☐ Truck.

2. What is the number of the plataform?
   ☐ 9 ¾ ☐ 9 ☐ 8 ¾ ☐ 934

3. Where is Harry going to?
   ☐ His friend's house.
   ☐ His house.
   ☐ Hogwarts.
   ☐ London.

4. What time does his means of transportation leave? At...
   ☐ 9:00 ☐ 12:00 ☐ 10:00 ☐ 11:00

LET'S PLAY

1 Read and paste the stickers of the means of transportation.

a) I would like to travel by air. I can see the clouds!

b) I would like to travel with my family by land. We can sing songs!

c) I would like to travel by water. It's very exciting!

2 Complete the sentence about yourself.

I would like to travel by _____ in a _____.

AFTER THIS UNIT I CAN

Identify the means of transportation.

Identify adjectives and associate them with the means of transportation.

Identify places and parts of cities.

Identify preference for some means of transportation by using *I would like to...*

UNIT 6
AT THE SCHOOL CAFETERIA

VOCABULARY

Bite: mordida, pedaço.
Cheese: queijo.
Delicious: delicioso(a).
Guys: pessoal, galera.

Option(s): opção (opções).
Order (to order): pedir uma refeição.
Slice: fatia.
Want (to want): quero (querer).

COMPREHENSION

1 Write **T** (true) or **F** (false).

☐ There are not a lot of options to order for lunch.

☐ Two kids order pizza.

☐ Harry decides to eat a sandwich.

☐ The pizza does not look that good for Eloise.

2 Listen to the audio again and circle the correct word.

a) The students are at the **library**/**cafeteria**.

b) The students are having **lunch**/**fun**.

c) The food looks **bad**/**good**.

3 Look at the images and write the food names. Circle the food items that Harry, and Sophie ate for lunch at school.

a)
_____

b)
_____

c)
_____

d)
_____

e)
_____

f)
_____

LET'S PLAY

1 Draw a crazy breakfast according to the instructions.

- 4 slices of blue pizza;
- 5 red cookies;
- 3 green sandwiches;
- 6 black ice cream cones;
- 2 cups of purple coffee;
- 3 grey oranges.

GRAMMAR POINT

Adjectives

Adjectives express quality, quantity, or extent.
Examples:

Old man

Young man

Healthy food

Unhealthy food

Long train

Short train

Small house

Big house

Sweet strawberry

Bitter coffee

Pay attention! In English, the adjective comes **before** the noun.

LET'S PLAY

1 Circle the adjectives in the word bank below.

- curly
- happy
- delicious
- photo
- big
- fish
- tall
- colorful
- car

2 Circle the adjectives in the following sentences.

a) This is a big pizza.
b) That is a small city.
c) This is an old house.
d) That is a blue ice cream cone.
e) I want a chocolate cookie.
f) This is an unhealthy meal.
g) I see a long train.
h) This is a bitter coffee.

LET'S LISTEN

1 Listen to the audio. Then complete the sentences with the correct adjective.

curly ✶ tall ✶ big ✶ colorful ✶ delicious ✶ happy

a) George has short and _____ hair.
b) That is a _____ tree. I can see it from far away.
c) My sister wants a _____ dress for the Carnival party!
d) My grandma cooks _____ meals.
e) _____ people smile all the time.
f) This is a _____ ball to play baseball!

LET'S PLAY

1 Circle the best adjective to describe each item below.

Ten green bottles

LET'S SING!

TEN green bottles **hanging** on the **wall**, (2x)
And if one green **bottle accidentally falls**, there'll be…
NINE green bottles hanging on the wall, (3x)
And if one green bottle accidentally falls, **there'll be**…
EIGHT green bottles hanging on the wall, (3x)
And if one green bottle accidentally falls, there'll be…
SEVEN green bottles hanging on the wall, (3x)
And if one green bottle accidentally falls, there'll be…
SIX green bottles hanging on the wall, (3x)
And if one green bottle accidentally falls, there'll be…
FIVE green bottles hanging on the wall, (3x)
And if one green bottle accidentally falls, there'll be…
FOUR green bottles hanging on the wall, (3x)
And if one green bottle accidentally falls, there'll be…
THREE green bottles hanging on the wall, (3x)
And if one green bottle accidentally falls, there'll be…
TWO green bottles hanging on the wall, (3x)
And if one green bottle accidentally falls, there'll be…
ONE green bottle hanging on the wall, (3x)
And if one green bottle should accidentally fall,
There'll be… no green bottles hanging on the wall!

Nursery rhyme. Adapted.

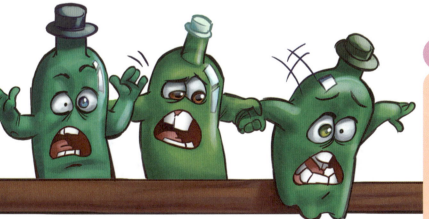

VOCABULARY

Accidentally: acidentalmente.
Bottle(s): garrafa(s).
Falls (to fall): cair.
Hanging (to hang): pendurada(s) (pendurar).
There will be (There to be): haverá (haver).
Wall: parede.

EIGHTY-ONE 81

DIGITAL PLAY

The different food items around the world

Japan

Germany

The USA

Brazil

France

Australia

Choose a country and research about its typical food. Write a sentence to introduce and describe its typical food.

_____
_____

ENGLISH AROUND THE WORLD

Cultural characteristics about food in schools around the world

Read the sentences and mark **T** (True) or **F** (False).

- ☐ Students eat breakfast and lunch in American school cafeterias.
- ☐ In Canada, students who have food allergies must wear bracelets.
- ☐ In Japan, after classes and lunch, students don't rest or clean the school.

GOOD DEED

A better school for a better world

Observe the image. Then write two words that would help to make a better school to create a better world.

_____

EIGHTY-THREE **83**

LET'S LISTEN

1 Listen and complete the blanks using the words from the box.

juice * breakfast * coffee * delicious * bacon * milk

Matt: Do you know the Brazilian _____, Andy?

Andy: No, I don't. How is it?

Matt: Well, we eat a piece of bread with butter, _____, _____, and _____ every day.

Andy: It looks _____!

Matt: It is!

Andy: Do you know what English people usually eat for breakfast? Eggs, _____, bread...

Matt: Really? I want to try.

2 Answer the questions about their breakfast.

a) Does Andy know the Brazilian breakfast?
_____

b) Did Matt eat the English breakfast?
_____

📖 LITERARY TIME

Let's read the comic strip!

🔍 VOCABULARY

I have eaten (I've eaten): eu comi.
It has been (It's been): tem sido.
Let's see: vejamos.

1 What meal does Garfield eat in the comic strip?
- [ ] Breakfast.
- [ ] Lunch.
- [ ] Dinner.

2 What does Garfield say about his morning?
- [ ] It's been a bad morning.
- [ ] It's been a good morning.

3 What is the number Garfield does with his paw?
- [ ] One.
- [ ] Two.
- [ ] Three.

4 Garfield is…
- [ ] Sad.
- [ ] Happy.

LET'S PLAY

1 Paste the sticker in the corresponding food or beverage item.

Juice	Coffee	Water
Milk	Meat	Chicken
Fish	Pizza	Grapes
Cheese	Apple	Strawberry

AFTER THIS UNIT I CAN

Identify different types of food.

Identify and use adjectives associated with food.

Understand the importance of respecting different cultures and their traditions.

Identify the culture of different countries and how food works in schools.

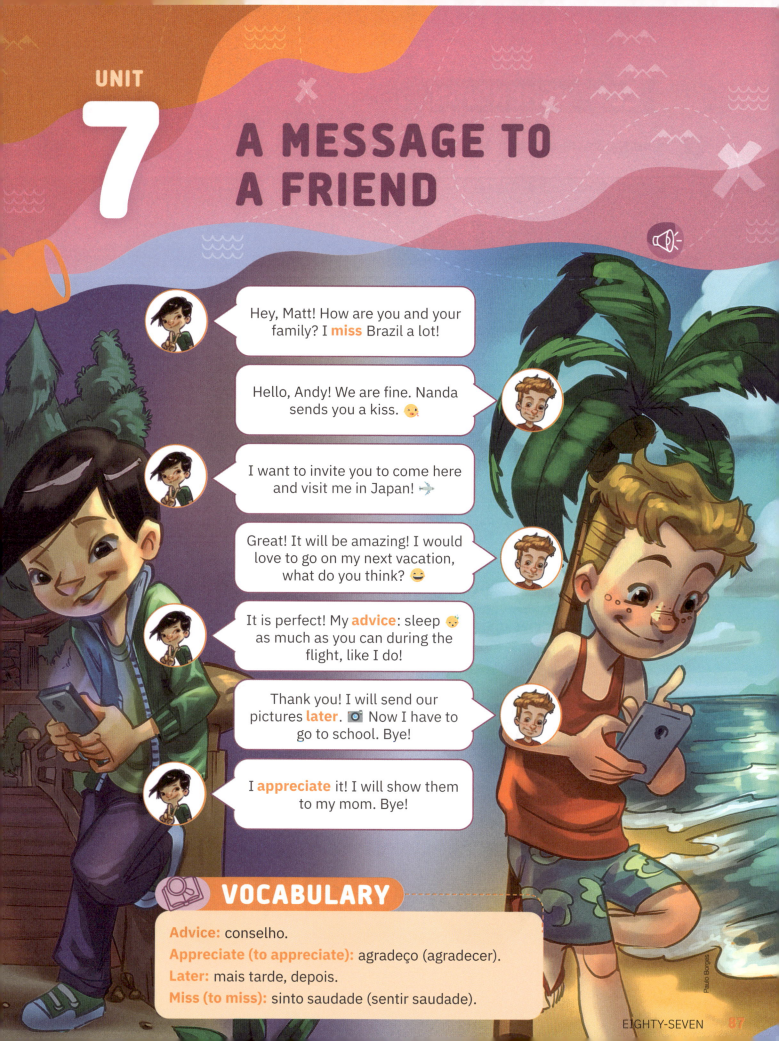

COMPREHENSION

1 Read the sentences and write True (**T**) or False (**F**).

a) Matt and Andy live in very far places.
☐ True   ☐ False

b) Andy was invited to visit Japan.
☐ True   ☐ False

c) Matt will not send the pictures to Andy.
☐ True   ☐ False

d) Andy is missing Brazil.
☐ True   ☐ False

2 Where is Matt going?
_____

3 Does Andy sleep during the flight to Japan?
_____

4 Look at these feelings and circle how you are feeling today.

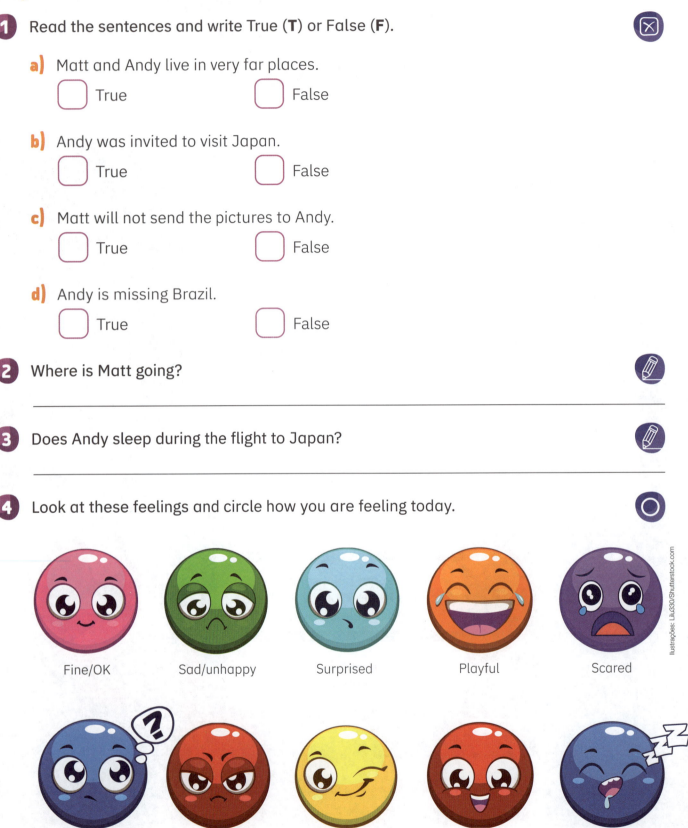

Fine/OK   Sad/unhappy   Surprised   Playful   Scared

Confused   Angry   Confident   Happy   Sleepy/tired

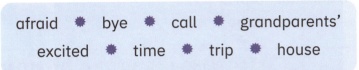

LET'S PLAY

1 Chloe sent an e-mail full of emojis to Harry. Can you decipher what she is saying? Use the words from the box.

> afraid * bye * call * grandparents'
> excited * time * trip * house

New message

recipient   harry@email.com

subject   Our next vacation!

Hey, Harry!

What 🕐 (time) is our ✈️ (trip) to your 👴👵 🏠 (grandparents' house)?

I am 😨 (afraid) to be late! Can you ☎️ (call) me?

I am 😄 (excited) about our ✈️ (trip).

👋 (bye)

Chloe

2 Answer the questions about Chloe's e-mail.

a) What does Chloe want to know? Mark with an **X**.

☐ The time of their trip.

☐ The place where they are going.

b) How is Chloe feeling about the trip? Circle it.

Happy

Scared

Sad

EIGHTY-NINE

ABC GRAMMAR POINT

Verb TO BE

Affirmative, negative, and question forms.
Let's remember how to use the verb **to be**.

Affirmative	Negative	Question
I **am** happy.	I **am not** happy.	**Am** I happy?
You **are** confused.	You **are not** confused.	**Are** you confused?
She **is** sad.	She **is not** sad.	**Is** she sad?
We **are** sleepy.	We **are not** sleepy.	**Are** we sleepy?
They **are** playful.	They **are not** playful.	**Are** they playful?

LET'S PLAY

1 Listen and complete the sentences with **am**, **is**, or **are**.

a) _____ you sick?

b) _____ Abbie sleepy?

c) Susan and Rick _____ happy.

d) You _____ fine.

e) She _____ not fine.

f) I _____ intelligent.

g) _____ Noah sad?

h) _____ the cat hungry?

2 How do they feel? Paste the sticker in the correct emotion.

surprised

playful

happy

thoughtful

confused

sad

scared

angry

LET'S SING!

Feelings poem

When I am sad, I want to **cry**.
When I am **proud**, I want to **fly**.
When I am **curious**, I want to **know**.
When I am **impatient**, I want to go.
When I am **bored**, I want to play.
When I am happy, I smile all day.
When I am **shy**, I want to **hide**.
When I'm **depressed**, I **stay inside**.
When I am **puzzled**, I want to **shrug**.
When I am loving, I kiss and **hug**.

Traditional poem.

VOCABULARY

Bored: entediado(a).
Cry (to cry): chorar.
Curious: curioso(a).
Depressed: triste, deprimido(a).
Fly (to fly): voar.
Hide (to hide): esconder.
Hug (to hug): abraçar.
Impatient: impaciente.

Inside: dentro.
Know (to know): conhecer, saber.
Proud: orgulhoso(a).
Puzzled: confuso(a).
Shrug (to shrug): encolher os ombros em sinal de dúvida.
Shy: tímido(a).
Stay (to stay): fico (ficar).

92 NINETY-TWO

LET'S PLAY

1 Rearrange the words to form questions. Follow the example.

> ✳ is / at home / your mother / ?
> Is your mother at home?

a) worried / are / your parents / ?
_____

b) the students / are / excited today / ?
_____

c) is / near here / the hospital / ?
_____

2 How are they feeling? Follow the example and write sentences about the character's feelings. Then rewrite these sentences in the negative form.

> ✳ She is sad. ⟶ She is not sad.

a)
_____
_____

b)
_____
_____

c)
_____
_____

d)
_____
_____

LITERARY TIME

Sunday 01

"**Once again**, Mom **committed** Dinner against the **entire** family tonight. [...]

Dad and I have been trying not to **complain** about the food. [...]

Since it's Sunday, **Dumb** Diary, I have to work on the homework that's due tomorrow **instead of sitting** on the couch **watching reruns** of reality TV shows, which is what I'd like to be doing. [...]

Anyway, we're **finishing up** our poetry unit in English class right now, and I have to write a poem about feelings. Here's what I have so far:

Mother dear, you've helped me grow
Into a pretty blossom.
So now I'd really like to know
Why you would feed me **possum**. [...]"

Jim Benton. *Dear dumb diary*: Am I the princess or the frog? London: Penguin Books, 2011. p. 2-3 and 5.

VOCABULARY

Anyway: de qualquer forma.
Committed (to commit): cometeu (cometer).
Complain (to complain): reclamar.
Dumb: pateta, estúpido.
Entire: inteira.
Finishing up (to finish up): terminando (terminar).

Instead of: em vez de.
Once again: novamente.
Possum: gambá.
Rerun(s): reprise(s).
Sitting (to sit): sentar-se.
Watching (to watch): assistindo (assistir).

1 How does the narrator feel about her mother's food?
- [ ] She likes it.
- [ ] She doesn't like it.

2 What is the homework about?
- [ ] A poem about her mother's food.
- [ ] A poem about her feelings.

ENGLISH AROUND THE WORLD

Art and feelings

Edvard Munch. *O grito*, 1893. Óleo, têmpera e pastel em cartão, 91 cm × 73,5 cm. Galeria Nacional de Oslo, na Noruega.

Let's draw our feelings!

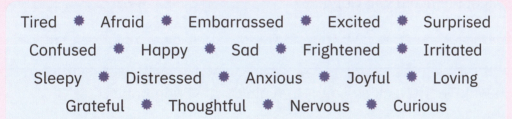

Tired * Afraid * Embarrassed * Excited * Surprised
Confused * Happy * Sad * Frightened * Irritated
Sleepy * Distressed * Anxious * Joyful * Loving
Grateful * Thoughtful * Nervous * Curious

DIGITAL PLAY

Let's browse and explore art and its feelings!

Vincent van Gogh. *A noite estrelada*, 1889. Óleo sobre tela, 73 cm × 92 cm. Museu de Arte Moderna de Nova York, Estados Unidos.

Research some famous paintings and write down the feelings they express.

a) The Starry Night – Vincent van Gogh.

_____
_____

b) Self-Portrait with Thorn Necklace and Hummingbird – Frida Kahlo.

_____
_____

AFTER THIS UNIT I CAN

Talk about the other person.

Identify feelings.

Identify adjectives.

Identify and use the present simple tense of verbs in affirmative, negative, and interrogative forms.

Reflect on art as a human manifestation of feelings.

Perceive the work as multicultural heritage.

UNIT 8
TRAVELING WITH FRIENDS

- The camp has a lot of **outdoor activities**.
- I love camping!
- There are activities like **canoeing**, **fishing**, and **climbing walls**.
- It is **wonderful** that we can **travel together** to the **scout's camp**!
- They also **organize** an **adventure course** and **nature trails**!

VOCABULARY

Activities: atividades.
Adventure course: percurso de aventura.
Canoeing: canoagem.
Climbing walls: escalada de paredes.
Fishing: pescaria.
Nature trail(s): trilha(s) na natureza.
Organize (to organize): organizam (organizar).
Outdoor: ao ar livre.
Scout's camp: acampamento de escoteiro.
Together: juntos.
Travel (to travel): viajar.
Wonderful: maravilhoso.

COMPREHENSION

1 What are Sophie, Oliver, Eloise, and George doing?

_____

2 What kind of activities does the camp offer?
- [ ] Indoor activities.
- [ ] Outdoor activities.

3 Which activities do the characters mention? Mark the images with an **X**.

- [ ] canoeing
- [ ] mountain biking
- [ ] fishing
- [ ] caving

- [ ] climbing walls
- [ ] cooking
- [ ] adventure course
- [ ] ladder climbing

- [ ] nature trails
- [ ] sailing
- [ ] pedal go-kart
- [ ] archery

GRAMMAR POINT

Adjectives

The **adjective** usually comes before the noun or pronoun it qualifies.

big
This is a **big** apple.

small
This is a **small** apple.

quiet
She is a **quiet** girl.

noisy
He is a **noisy** boy.

long
This is a **long** hair.

short
This is a **short** hair.

fast
It is a **fast** rabbit.

slow
It is a **slow** turtle.

interesting
It is an **interesting** school day.

boring
It is a **boring** day.

beautiful
It is a **beautiful** teddy bear.

ugly
It is an **ugly** teddy bear.

dangerous
This is a **dangerous** hobby.

safe
This is a **safe** helmet.

strong
The man with brown hair is a **strong** man.

weak
The man with red hair is a **weak** man.

LET'S PLAY

1 Let's practice the use of adjectives. Choose the best option to each image.

a)

☐ beautiful   ☐ ugly

b)

☐ hot   ☐ cold

GOOD DEED

There are many beautiful places in the world

There are cities, the countryside, beaches, and mountains... We have to take care of all these places if we want them to exist for many and many years!

How can you help to preserve nature and the environment?
_____

LET'S LISTEN

1 Listen and read the activities Matt, Evie, Andy, and Abbie want to do on their next trip. Then, circle these activities.

a)  We can play frisbee.

b)  We can sunbathe.

c)  We can build sandcastles.

d)  We can look for seashells.

✸ Now, answer: Where do they want to travel?

_____

DIGITAL PLAY

The famous New York touristic bus

Research and mark the correct alternatives according to the Big Bus Tours USA.

- [ ] Two kinds of bus: closed and no roof.
- [ ] 3 kinds of tickets.
- [ ] 15% discount advanced tickets.

ENGLISH AROUND THE WORLD

The fascinating Kennedy Space Center Visitor Complex

1 How far is the Kennedy Space Center Visitor Complex, Florida from Orlando, Florida? (in minutes)

_____

2 What is the name of the space bus that you can see at Kennedy Space Center Visitor Complex in Cape Canaveral?

_____

The bear went over the mountain

Oh the bear went over the mountain,
the bear went over the mountain,
the bear went over the mountain,
to see what he could see.

Chorus
But all that he could see,
but all that he could see,
was the other side of the mountain,
the other side of the mountain,
the other side of the mountain,
was all that he could see.

So he went back over the mountain,
he went back over the mountain,
he went back over the mountain,
to see what he could see.

Nursery rhyme.

LET'S SING!

VOCABULARY

Bear: urso.
Mountain: montanha.
Other: outro.
Over: por cima.
See (to see): ver.
Side: lado.
Went back (to go back): voltou (voltar).

📖 LITERARY TIME

Diary of a wimpy kid: the last straw

"[...] Monday I **figure** the best **way** to get Dad to **forget** that father-son camping **mess** is to have a **do-over**. So **tonight** at dinner, I asked Dad if he wanted to go on a camping **trip**, just me and him.

I've been **studying** up on my Boy Scouts manual, and I'm pretty **eager** to **show off** what **I've learned**. [...]"

Jeff Kinney. *Diary of a wimpy kid: the last straw.* New York: Amulet Books, 2009. p. 368.

🔍 VOCABULARY

Do-over: fazer outra vez, novamente.
Eager: ansioso.
Figure (to figure): imagino (imaginar).
Forget (to forget): esquecer.
I have learned (to learn): aprendi (aprender).
Mess: bagunça.
Show off (to show off): exibir-se.
Studying (to study): estudando (estudar).
Tonight: esta noite.
Trip: viagem.
Way: jeito.
Wimpy: fracote, banana.

1 Where are they going? Circle it.

To the beach.   To a campsite.

2 When did he make the suggestion to his dad? Circle it.

During breakfast.   During lunch.   During dinner.

LET'S PLAY

1 What sports do you like the most? Write and paste the stickers in the order you like them.

My favorite sports	
1st: _____	
2nd: _____	
3rd: _____	
4th: _____	
5th: _____	

2 Look at the pictures and match them with the adjectives.

a) fast

b) quiet

c) dangerous

d) small

ONE HUNDRED FIVE **105**

LET'S HAVE FUN

1 Look at the pictures and find ten differences.

AFTER THIS UNIT I CAN

	🙂	😐	☹️
Use the verb *can*.			
Identify adjectives.			
Identify different kinds of sports and adventure activities.			
Identify the antonyms of adjectives.			
Value the world's space history.			
Identify transport strategies for visiting a tourist city.			

106   ONE HUNDRED SIX

REVIEW

Unit 1

1 Let's play bingo!

Awesome * Dress * Guitar * Kite * Near * Rice
Teacher * Backpack * Ear * English * Geography * Nurse
Running * Underwear * Baker * Engineer * Hamburger
Lunch * Owl * Sandals * Vacation * Body * Flute
History * Machine * Pants * Shirt * Yogurt * Cycling
Friendship * Ice cream * Money * Pencil case * Spring
Cheese * Fruits * Judge * Museum * Pilot * Tea

ONE HUNDRED SEVEN **107**

Unit 2

1 What season of the year is it? Write.

Fall • Winter • Summer • Spring

a)

_____

c)

_____

b)

_____

d)

_____

2 What's your favorite season of the year? Draw and write.

_____

3 Look at the pictures and complete the sentences with the verb **to be**.

a)

He _____ happy. He is angry.

b)

They _____ magazines. They are books.

c)

I _____ warm. I am cold.

d)

It _____ winter. It is spring.

e)

They _____ hungry. They are bored.

Unit 3

1 Look at the map and find out some places in the neighborhood. Complete the sentences using the prepositions of place from the box.

on * in front of * between * next to

a) The library is _____ the museum.

b) The drugstore is _____ the supermarket.

c) The stores are _____ the park and the supermarket.

d) The movie theater is _____ the same street of the school.

2 Write the direction each traffic sign indicates.

a)

_____

b)

_____

c)

_____

3 What places are these? Read and match the pictures with the names.

a) Bakery

b) Library

c) Museum

d) Store

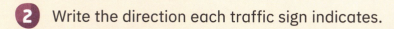

Unit 4

1 Unscramble the letters and find the names of family members. Then write them on the picture.

a) retghuad
_____

b) celnu
_____

c) tnua
_____

d) rethfa
_____

e) dnrgarethmo
_____

f) nos
_____

g) erthom
_____

h) erthafdnrag
_____

Unit 5

1 Look at the images. Complete the crossword puzzle with the corresponding means of transportation.

subway * ferry * train * motorcycle * truck * helicopter * car * plane

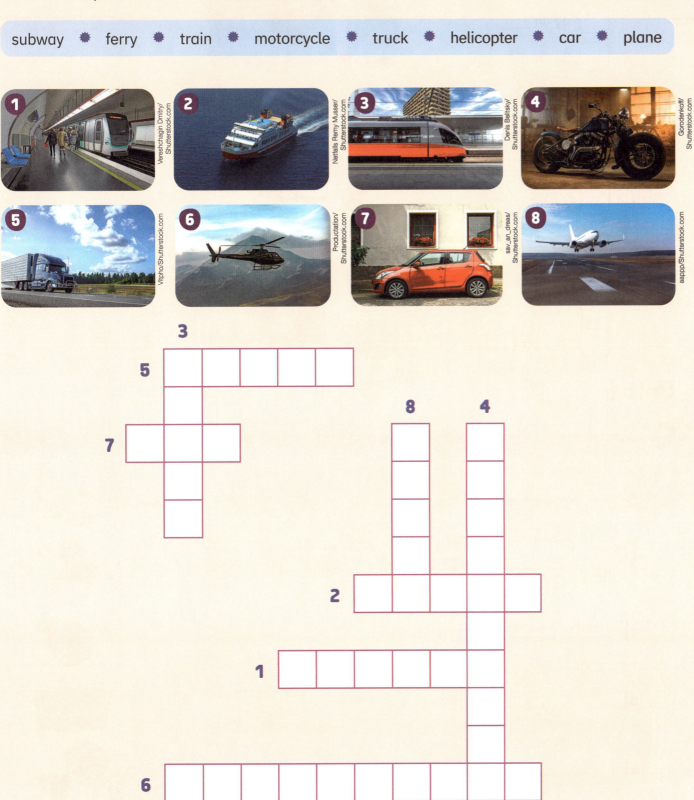

2 Observe the images and mark the correct option.

a) The Minions need a helicopter.
- ☐ By land
- ☐ By air
- ☐ By water

b) The Minions need a motorcycle.
- ☐ By land
- ☐ By air
- ☐ By water

c) The Minions need a boat.
- ☐ By land
- ☐ By air
- ☐ By water

Unit 6

1 Complete the sentences with **a** or **an** and match them with the correct image.

a) _____ apple.

b) _____ dog.

c) _____ English book.

d) _____ banana.

e) _____ delicious ice cream.

2 Complete the sentences with the correct adjective from the box.

> young * delicious * unhealthy * bitter * sweet

a) An example of an _____ lunch is a hamburger and French fries.

b) My sister is only 5 years old. She is _____.

c) I don't like _____ juices. I always put sugar in them.

d) My mom loves fruit salad! She says it's _____!

e) In the morning, I like to eat _____ fruits.

3 Look at the food and beverage in the box. Put them in the correct category.

> chicken sandwich * pizza * soup * fruit salad * cookies
> juice * bacon * milk * fish * cereal * coffee * water
> grapes * strawberry * meat * bread * apple

Beverage	Food
_____	_____
_____	_____
_____	_____

4 What do you like to have for breakfast? Using the items from activity 2, draw and write a perfect breakfast.

ONE HUNDRED FIFTEEN **115**

Unit 7

1 How is he feeling? Look at the images and answer.

a)

d)

b)

e)

c)

f)

2 Complete the sentences with **am**, **is** or **are**.

a) _____ Evie hungry?

b) Eloise and Harry _____ sleepy.

c) _____ you happy?

d) Sophie _____ not sad.

e) I _____ confused.

f) _____ the dog playful?

g) _____ they sick?

h) Jim and Tom _____ not scared.

3 Draw the emotions.

Happy

Sad

Surprised

Angry

Unit 8

1 Look at the pictures. Then complete the Camping Trip crossword puzzle with the words from the box.

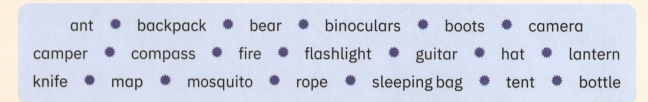

ant * backpack * bear * binoculars * boots * camera
camper * compass * fire * flashlight * guitar * hat * lantern
knife * map * mosquito * rope * sleeping bag * tent * bottle

2 Read and complete with an adjective from the box.

> small ✻ dangerous ✻ interesting ✻ strong ✻ noisy

a) Ann's favorite subject is Math. She thinks it's _____.

b) Carnival is a _____ celebration.

c) Riding a bike without a helmet is _____.

d) Jim plays sports to be healthy and _____.

e) Ladybugs are _____ insects.

3 Find and circle 7 outdoor activities in the wordsearch.

GLOSSARY

A few days: uns dias, alguns dias
Accidentally: acidentalmente
Activity: atividade
Adorn: enfeite
Adorn, to: enfeitar
Adventure course: percurso de aventura
Advice: conselho
Air: ar
Angry: bravo(a)
Another: outro(a)
Ant: formiga
Anxious: ansioso(a)
Any: algum(a)
Anything: qualquer coisa
Anyway: de qualquer forma
Appreciate, to: agradecer

Archery: arqueiro
Archway: arco
Aunt: tia
Autumn: outono
Away: longe
Awesome: incrível

Bacon: toucinho
Balloon: balão
Barrier: barreira
Be late, to: estar atrasado(a)
Beach: praia
Bear: urso
Bear, to: carregar
Beautiful: bonito(a)
Before: antes
Behind: atrás
Beverage: bebida
Bicycle: bicicleta
Big: grande
Bite: mordida, pedaço
Bitter: amargo
Bloom, to: florescer
Boat: barco
Bored: entediado(a)
Boring: chato(a)
Borrow, to: pedir emprestado
Bother, to: incomodar-se
Bottle: garrafa
Brazilian: brasileiro(a)
Bread: pão
Breakfast: café da manhã
Bright: claro
Brother: irmão
Browse, to: navegar
Bus: ônibus

Butter: manteiga
Buy, to: comprar

Can: poder, conseguir
Canoe: canoa
Canoeing: canoagem
Canvas: tela
Car: carro
Caving: passeio em caverna
Character: personagem
Chat, to: conversar
Cheese: queijo
Chicken: frango
City: cidade
Climb, to: escalar
Climbing walls: escalada de paredes
Coffee: café
Cold: frio
Colorful: colorido
Come out, to: sair
Commit, to: cometer
Complain, to: reclamar
Confident: confiante
Confused: confuso(a)

Contemplative: contemplativo(a)
Cookie: biscoito
Cooking: cozinhar
Cousin: primo(a)
Crash, to: estrondear
Cry, to: chorar
Curious: curioso(a)

Curly: cacheado

 D

Dance, to: dançar
Dangerous: perigoso(a)
Delicious: delicioso(a)
Depressed: triste, deprimido(a)
Deserve, to: merecer
Die, to: morrer
Dislike, to: não gostar
Distressed: irritado(a)
Do-over, to: fazer outra vez, novamente
Domestic: doméstico
Draw, to: desenhar

Drip, to: gotejar

Driver: motorista
Dumb: pateta, bobo(a)

 E

Eager: ansioso(a)

Ear of corn: espiga de milho
Eat, to: comer
Eco-airplane: avião ecológico
Egg: ovo
Elder: idoso(a)
Embarrassed: envergonhado(a)
Enjoy, to: gostar, curtir
Entire: inteiro(a)
Environment: meio ambiente
Excited: animado(a)
Exciting: emocionante
Explore, to: explorar

 F

Fable: fábula
Fall: outono
Fall, to: cair
Fare: passagem
Fascinating: fascinante
Fast: rápido
Fat: gordura, gorduroso(a)
Father: pai
Ferry: balsa
Field: campo

Figure, to: imaginar
Fine: bem
Finish up, to: acabar, terminar
First: primeiro(a)
Fish (to fish): pesca (pescar)

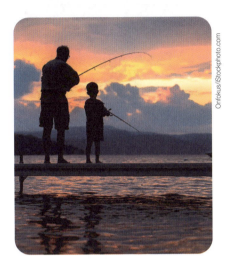

Fishing: pescaria
Fly, to: voar
Flyer: folheto
Food: comida
Forget, to: esquecer
Free: livre
Friendship: amizade
Frightened: assustado(a)
Fruit: fruta
Fun: diversão

 G

Get to, to: chegar a
Get to know, to: conhecer
Gloves: luvas
Go back, to: voltar
Go round, to: girar

ONE HUNDRED TWENTY-ONE **121**

Go straight, to: ir em frente
Grandfather: avô
Grandma: vovó
Grandmother: avó
Grandpa: vovô
Grandparents: avós
Grasshopper: gafanhoto
Grateful: grato(a)
Great-aunt: tia-avó
Guys: pessoal, galera

Had done it: conseguiu
Halfpenny: moeda britânica de meio centavo, não é mais usada desde 1984
Hamburger: hambúrguer
Hang, to: pendurar
Happy: feliz
Have learned, to: aprender
Healthy: saudável
Heavy: pesado(a)
Helicopter: helicóptero
Hide, to: esconder
Hop about, to: saltitar
Hot: quente

Hot-air balloon: balão de ar quente
Hug, to: abraçar
Hunger: fome

I can't wait: mal posso esperar
Imagination: imaginação
Impatient: impaciente
Improve, to: melhorar
In line: em fila
Inside: dentro
Instead of: em vez de
Interesting: interessante
Introduce, to: apresentar
Invite: convite

Invite, to: convidar

It's been (to be): tem sido (ser, estar)
I've eaten (to eat): comi (comer)

Joyful: alegre

Juice: suco
Junk: não saudável

Kind: gentil
Kindness: bondade
Know, to: conhecer

Ladder: escada
Ladder climbing: escalada de escada
Lake: lago
Land: terra
Laptop: *laptop*, computador portátil
Later: mais tarde
Lay up, to: juntar
Leave, to: sair, deixar

Leaves: folhas
Leisure: lazer
Let's see: vejamos
Library: biblioteca
Long: longo(a), comprido(a)
Look, to: olhar
Love, to: amar
Loving: amoroso(a)

Meal: refeição
Means of transportation: meio(s) de transporte
Meet, to: encontrar
Melt, to: derreter
Mess: bagunça
Message: mensagem
Milk: leite
Miss, to: sentir falta

Moon: Lua

Mother: mãe
Motorbike/motorcycle: motocicleta
Mountain: montanha
Move, to: mover (mover-se)
Movies: filmes/cinema
Museum: museu

Nature trail: trilha na natureza
Near: ao lado de/do/da
Necessity: necessidade
Neighborhood: bairro, vizinhança
Nephew: sobrinho
Nervous: nervoso(a)
Network: redes sociais
Nice to meet you: prazer em conhecê-lo(la)
Niece: sobrinha
No way: nem pensar
Not that good: não tão bom

Oatmeal: mingau
Of course: claro
Old: velho(a)
Once again: novamente, de novo
Open, to: abrir
Option: opção
Order, to: pedir uma refeição
Organize, to: organizar
Other: outro
Outdoor: ao ar livre
Overhead: aéreo, acima da cabeça

Packed (to pack with): amontoado(a), lotado(a) (amontoar, lotar)
Paint: pintura
Paint, to: pintar
Park: parque
Pass by, to: passar por
Pedal go-kart: *kart* de pedal
Plan: plano
Plan, to: planejar
Plane: avião
Playfellow: amigo(a), companheiro(a) de brincadeiras

Playful: brincalhão/brincalhona
Plenty: bastante, em abundância
Politeness: educação, cortesia
Pollute, to: poluir
Possum: gambá
Practice, to: praticar
Prefer, to: preferir
Previous: anterior
Proud: orgulhoso(a)

Puzzle pieces: peças de quebra-cabeça/enigma
Puzzled: confuso(a)

R

Really: realmente
Relationship: relacionamento
Relative: parente
Relaxing: relaxante
Rerun: reprise

Roller skate, to: andar de patins

Roof: teto
Rudeness: má educação, grosseria

S

Sad: triste
Safe: seguro(a)
Sail, to: velejar
Salad: salada
Sandcastle: castelo de areia
Sandwich: sanduíche
Save, to: economizar, salvar
Say, to: dizer
Scared: assustado(a)
Scarlet: escarlate, vermelho
Scout: escoteiro(a)
Scout's camp: acampamento de escoteiros
Seashell: concha
Season: estação do ano
See, to: ver
Seem to be (expressão): parecer
Selfishness: egoísmo
Ship: navio
Shine, to: brilhar
Short: pequeno(a), baixo(a), curto(a)
Show, to: mostrar
Show off, to: mostrar-se, exibir-se
Shrug, to: encolher os ombros em sinal de dúvida
Shy: tímido(a)
Side: lado
Sigh: suspiro
Sister: irmã
Sit, to: sentar-se
Skill: habilidade
Sky: céu

Sleep: sono
Sleep, to: dormir
Sleepy: sonolento(a)
Slice: pedaço
Slow: devagar/lento(a)
Small: pequeno(a)
Snack bar: lanchonete
Snow: neve
Snowman: boneco de neve
Someday: algum dia
Sorcerer: feiticeiro(a), mágico(a)
Soup: sopa
Speedboat: lancha
Spider: aranha
Splash, to: borrifar
Spring: primavera
Surprised: surpreso(a)
Sustainable: sustentável
Stand up, to: ficar de pé, levantar-se
Stay, to: ficar

Steam engine: locomotiva a vapor
Street: rua
Strong: forte
Study up, to: estudar
Subway: metrô
Summer: verão
Sunbathe, to: tomar sol
Supper: jantar, ceia

Sure: claro
Sweet: doce
Sweety: doce/docinho
Swish, to: balançar, mover-se com um som suave

Teach, to: ensinar
There to be: haver
Thoughtful: pensativo(a)
Three-quarters: três quartos
Through: através
Thunder: trovão
Time: tempo
Tired: cansado(a)
Together: juntos(as)
Tomato: tomate
Tonight: esta noite
Train: trem
Travel, to: viajar
Trip: viagem

Truck: caminhão
Tummy: barriga
Turn left, to: virar à esquerda
Turn right, to: virar à direita

Ugly: feio(a)
Uncle: tio

Unhappy: infeliz
Unhealthy: não saudável

Vacation: férias

Wall: muro, parede
Walk, to: andar

Walk down, to: caminhar por
Want, to: querer
Warm: quente
Warn, to: alertar
Waste: desperdício
Waste, to: desperdiçar
Watch, to: assistir
Water: água
Way: jeito
Weak: fraco(a)
Weather: clima, tempo
Wheel: roda
Wild: selvagem
Wimpy: fracote, banana
Winter: inverno
Wiper: limpador de para-brisa
Wisdom: sabedoria
Whoop: uhul (grito de comemoração)
Wonderful: maravilhoso
Work hard, to: trabalhar duro
Worried: preocupado(a)
Worry, to: preocupar-se
Would like: gostaria
Wrought iron: ferro forjado

Young: jovem

INDEX

SONGS

UNIT 1 Girls and boys come out to play — **26**
UNIT 2 Five little snowmen — **37**
UNIT 3 Rig a jig jig — **47**
UNIT 4 Grandma's house — **56**
UNIT 5 The wheels on the bus — **69**
UNIT 6 Ten green bottles — **81**
UNIT 7 Feelings poem — **92**
UNIT 8 The bear went over the mountain — **103**

LISTENINGS

UNIT 1
Fun, hobbies, and games! — **19**
Hobbies — **28**
Whose hobby is this? — **28**

UNIT 2
The seasons of the year — **31**
The weather — **38**
Activities — **38**

UNIT 3
Different cities — **41**
The map — **43**
Giving directions — **44**

UNIT 4
Matt's family — **51**
Matt's e-mail — **57**
Matt's new e-mail — **59**

UNIT 5
Means of transportation — **63**
By land, air or water? — **68**
The park — **70**

UNIT 6
At the school cafeteria — **75**
Adjectives — **79**
Brazilian or American breakfast — **84**

UNIT 7
A message to a friend — **87**
Verb to be — **90**

UNIT 8
Traveling with friends — **97**
Where do they want to go? — **101**

Paulo Borges

ONE HUNDRED TWENTY-SEVEN **127**

CELEBRATIONS

Easter

Easter

Teacher's Day

International Family's Day

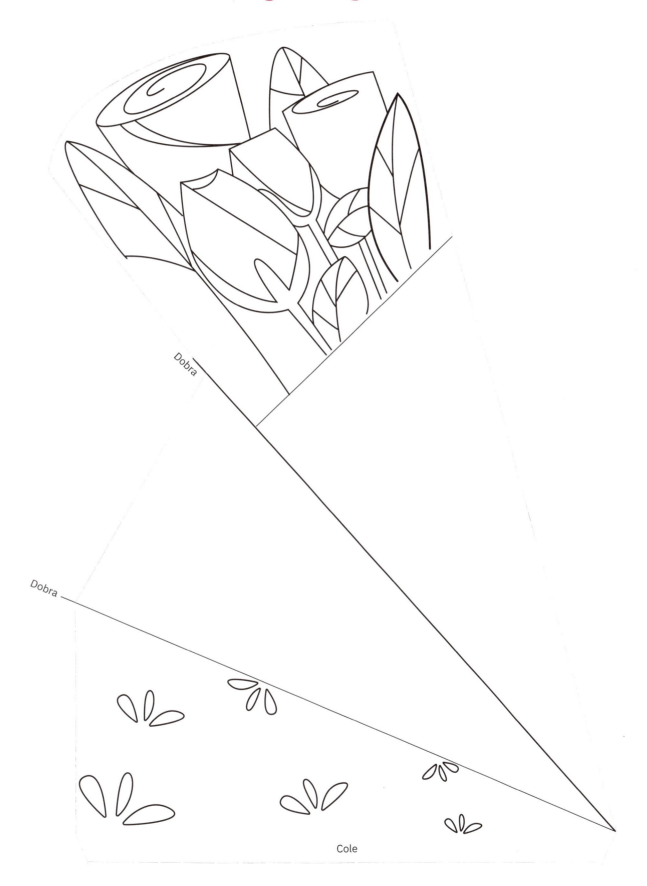

Children's Day

Thanksgiving

Dobra

Christmas

New Year's Eve

Let's start!
Page 9

STICKERS

Unit 1
Page 23

Unit 2
Page 33

ONE HUNDRED FORTY-FIVE 145

STICKERS

Unit 3
Page 46

Unit 4
Page 58

| grandfather | cousin | uncle | grandmother | aunt |

| aunt | cousin | grandfather | uncle | grandmother |

| sister | father | brother | mother |

STICKERS

Unit 5
Page 74

Unit 6
Page 86

Unit 7

Page 91

Unit 8

Page 105

ONE HUNDRED FIFTY-ONE 151